Afghan Parade

designed for crochet

INTRODUCTION

What could possibly be more cozy than snuggling up with a warm afghan, next to the fireplace, on a cold winter night? You'll find four distinctively different crocheted designs on the next few pages. Each afghan is worked in one piece (no seams to sew!) using worsted weight yarn. We've included photographs of two different color combinations for each style, but your imagination is your only limitation.

Barbara B. Rondeau

Design Department

Table of Contents

Leisure Arts Inc. • Maumelle Arkansas

SMALL SHELL

Finished Size: Approximately 50" x 73" (127 cm x 185.5 cm)

MATERIALS

Worsted Weight Yarn, approximately:
Solid Afghan - 60 ounces, (1,700 grams)

Variation 1
Main Color - 41 ounces, (1,160 grams)
Color A - 13 ounces, (370 grams)
Color B - 6 ounces, (170 grams)

Variation 2
Main Color - 46 ounces, (1,310 grams)
Contrasting Color - 14 ounces, (400 grams)

Crochet hook, size H (5 mm)
or size needed for gauge

GAUGE: 9 (sc, dc) groups = 5" (12.75 cm);
8 rows = 3" (7.5 cm)

INSTRUCTIONS

With Main Color, ch 170 **loosely**.

Row 1: (Sc, dc) in second ch from hook, ★ skip next ch, (sc, dc) in next ch; repeat from ★ across: 85 (sc, dc) groups.

Row 2: Ch 1, turn; (sc, dc) in each sc across.

Repeat Row 2 for pattern.

SOLID AFGHAN *(not photographed)*
Work a total of 188 rows.

VARIATION 1 *(shown below)*
Continuing with Main Color, work a total of 29 rows. At end of last row, work last dc until 2 loops remain on hook, cut yarn, with Color A finish dc ***(Fig. 5b, page 12)***.

Note: Change colors in same manner throughout.

Work in the following Color Sequence: 8 rows Color A, 8 rows Color B, 8 rows Color A, 29 rows Main Color. Repeat Color Sequence 2 times **more**.
Do **not** finish off or change color at end of last row.

Variation 1

VARIATION 2 *(shown below)*
Continuing with Main Color, work a total of 30 rows. At end of last row, work last dc until 2 loops remain on hook, cut yarn, with Contrasting Color finish dc ***(Fig. 5b, page 12)***.

Note: Change colors in same manner throughout.

Work in the following Color Sequence:
12 rows Contrasting Color, 6 rows Main Color,
12 rows Contrasting Color, 68 rows Main Color,
12 rows Contrasting Color, 6 rows Main Color,
12 rows Contrasting Color, 30 rows Main Color.
At end of last row change to Contrasting Color in last dc.

EDGING

Rnd 1: Ch 3 **(counts as first dc)**, 2 dc in same st (corner), working across side, skip first row, dc in edge of next 187 rows; working in free loops of beginning ch ***(Fig. 4, page 12)***, 3 dc in first ch, work 167 dc evenly spaced across to last ch, 3 dc in last ch; working across side, skip first row, dc in edge of next 187 rows; working in sts across top edge, 3 dc in first sc, work 167 dc evenly spaced across; join with slip st to third ch of beginning ch-3: 720 dc.

Rnd 2: Ch 3 **(counts as first dc)**, **†** 3 dc in next dc, dc in next 189 dc, 3 dc in next dc **†**, dc in next 169 dc; repeat from **†** to **†** once, dc in next 168 dc; join with slip st to third ch of beginning ch-3: 728 dc.

Rnd 3: Slip st in same st, hdc in next dc, 2 dc in next dc, hdc in next dc, ★ slip st in next dc, hdc in next dc, 2 dc in next dc, hdc in next dc; repeat from ★ around; join with slip st to first st, finish off.

Weave in all yarn ends.

Variation 2

V-STITCH SHELL

by Virginia Hogan; North Little Rock, AR

Finished Size: Approximately 48" x 73" (122 cm x 185.5 cm)

MATERIALS

Worsted Weight Yarn, approximately:

Solid Afghan - 42 ounces, (1,190 grams)

Striped Afghan

Main Color - 27 ounces, (770 grams)

Contrasting Color - 15 ounces, (430 grams)

Crochet hook, size J (6 mm) **or** size needed for gauge

GAUGE: 5 V-sts = 4" (10 cm); 3 V-st rows = 2" (5 cm)

Note: For Striped Afghan, work Rows 1-8 with Contrasting Color; finish off.
Join Main Color with slip st in last dc of Row 8, ch 4, turn.
Work Rows 9-22. Work remaining rows in the following sequence: (6 rows Contrasting Color, 14 rows Main Color) 4 times, 8 rows Contrasting Color.
Work Edging with Main Color.

INSTRUCTIONS

Ch 174 **loosely**.

Row 1: (Dc, ch 1, dc) **(V-st)** in fifth ch from hook, ★ skip next 2 chs, V-st in next ch; repeat from ★ across to last ch, dc in last ch: 57 V-sts.

Rows 2-10: Ch 4, turn; V-st in first V-st (ch-1 sp) and in each V-st across, dc in turning ch.

Note: To **Treble Crochet** *(abbreviated tr)*, YO twice, insert hook in st or sp indicated, YO and pull up a loop (4 loops on hook), (YO and draw through 2 loops on hook) 3 times.

Row 11 (Right side)**:** Ch 4, turn; V-st in first 3 V-sts, ★ skip next V-st, 9 tr in next V-st **(Shell made)**, skip next V-st, V-st in next 3 V-sts; repeat from ★ across, tr in turning ch: 9 Shells.

Row 12: Ch 4, turn; V-st in first 3 V-sts, ★ ch 4, sc in fifth tr of next Shell, ch 4, V-st in next 3 V-sts; repeat from ★ across, tr in turning ch: 30 V-sts.

Row 13: Ch 4, turn; V-st in first 3 V-sts, ★ Shell in next sc, V-st in next 3 V-sts; repeat from ★ across, tr in turning ch: 9 Shells.

Rows 14-20: Repeat Rows 12 and 13, 3 times; then repeat Row 12 once **more**.

Row 21: Ch 4, turn; V-st in first 3 V-sts, ★ V-st in next ch-4 sp, V-st in next sc, V-st in next ch-4 sp, V-st in next 3 V-sts; repeat from ★ across, dc in turning ch: 57 V-sts.

Rows 22-30: Ch 4, turn; V-st in first V-st (ch-1 sp) and in each V-st across, dc in turning ch.

Repeat Rows 11-30, 4 times **more**; do **not** finish off.

EDGING

With **right** side facing, skip first V-st, † 7-tr Shell in next V-st, sc in next V-st †; repeat from † to † across, sc in turning ch; working across side, (sc around next turning ch, 7-tr Shell around next dc or tr) across; working in bottom of V-sts (free loops of beginning ch) across bottom edge, sc in first V-st; repeat from † to † across; working across side, (7-tr Shell around next turning ch, sc around next dc or tr) across; join with slip st to first st, finish off.

Weave in all yarn ends.

Striped
Afghan

Scrap Afghan

LACY CHEVRON

by Sr. Mary F. Strecker CSJ; Manhattan, KS

Finished Size: Approximately 49" x 72" (124.5 cm x 183 cm)

MATERIALS

Worsted Weight Yarn, approximately:

Planned Afghan

Main Color - 19 ounces, (540 grams)
Color A - 15 ounces, (430 grams)
Colors B **and** C - 8 ounces, (230 grams) **each**

Scrap Afghan

Main Color - 11 ounces, (310 grams)
5 Contrasting Colors - 39 ounces, (1,110 grams) **total**

Crochet hook, size H (5 mm)
or size needed for gauge

GAUGE: One pattern repeat (from point to point) = 3¼" (8.25 cm); 8 rows = 5½" (14 cm)

INSTRUCTIONS

With Main Color, ch 286 **loosely**.

Row 1: Dc in third ch from hook, ch 2, skip next 3 chs, 2 dc in next ch, ch 2, skip next 3 chs, ★ † (2 dc, ch 2, 2 dc) in next ch (**Shell made**), ch 2, skip next 3 chs, 2 dc in next ch, ch 2, skip next 3 chs †, 2 dc in next ch, skip next 2 chs, (2 dc in next ch, ch 2, skip next 3 chs) twice; repeat from ★ 13 times **more**, then repeat from † to † **once**, dc in last 2 chs: 15 Shells.

Row 2: Ch 3, turn; working **over** the ch-2 of Row 1 (so that the ch-2 disappears into the dc) **AND** in the beginning ch, dc in first base ch (middle ch of next 3 skipped chs) ***(Fig. 1a)***, ★ † ch 2, 2 dc in next base ch, ch 2, work Shell in next Shell (ch-2 sp), ch 2, 2 dc in next base ch, ch 2 †, 2 dc in next base ch, do **not** work in next 2 skipped chs, 2 dc in next base ch; repeat from ★ 13 times **more**, then repeat from † to † once, dc in next base ch, dc in top of turning ch.

Fig. 1a

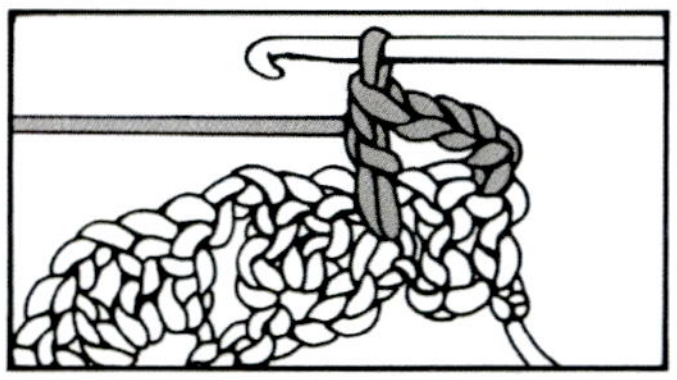

Planned Afghan

PLANNED AFGHAN *(shown on page 7)*
Row 3: Ch 3, turn; working **over** the ch-2 of previous row **AND** in center of 2-dc groups 2 rows **below**, dc in center of first 2-dc group, ch 2, ★ † 2 dc in center of next 2-dc group (in first half of Shell), ch 2, work Shell in next Shell of previous row ***(Fig. 1b)***, ch 2, 2 dc in center of next 2-dc group (in second half of Shell), ch 2 †, 2 dc in center of next 2-dc group, skip next two 2-dc groups, 2 dc in center of next 2-dc group, ch 2; repeat from ★ 13 times **more**, then repeat from † to † **once**, dc in center of next 2-dc group, dc in top of turning ch.

Rows 4-6: Repeat Row 3, 3 times **more**.

Finish off. Join Color A with slip st in last dc.

Repeat Row 3 working in the following Color Sequence: 5 rows Color A, 3 rows Color B, 3 rows Color C, 5 rows Main Color.
Repeat Color Sequence 5 times **more**. Do **not** finish off.

Fig. 1b

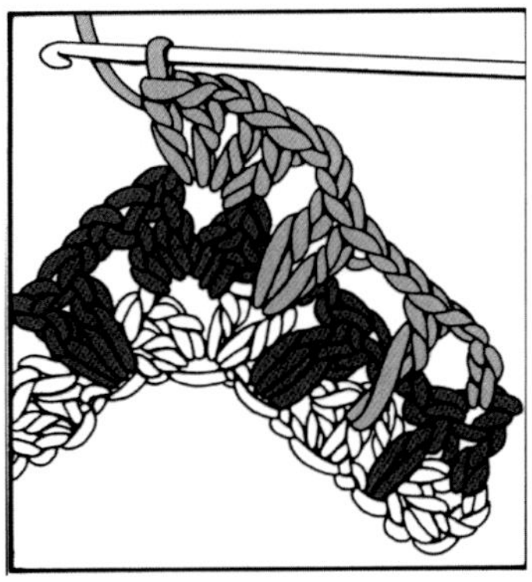

SCRAP AFGHAN *(shown on page 6)*
Finish off after Row 2. Join Color A with slip st in last dc.

Row 3: Ch 3, turn; working **over** ch-2 of previous row **AND** in center of 2-dc groups 2 rows **below**, dc in center of first 2-dc group, ch 2, ★ † 2 dc in center of next 2-dc group (in first half of Shell), ch 2, work Shell in next Shell of previous row ***(Fig. 1b)***, ch 2, 2 dc in center of next 2-dc group (in second half of Shell), ch 2 †, 2 dc in center of next 2-dc group, skip next two 2-dc groups, 2 dc in center of next 2-dc group, ch 2; repeat from ★ 13 times **more**, then repeat from † to † **once**, dc in center of next 2-dc group, dc in top of turning ch.

Row 4: Repeat Row 3. Finish off. Join next color with slip st in last dc.

Repeat Rows 3 and 4, working 2 rows of each color in the following Color Sequence: Color B, Color C, Color D, Color E, Main Color, A.
Repeat Color Sequence 7 times **more**, ending by working only one Main Color row. Do **not** finish off.

TOP EDGING

Row 1: Continuing with Main Color, ch 3, turn; dc in center of first 2-dc group 2 rows **below**, sc in next 2 dc of previous row, 2 dc in center of next 2-dc group 2 rows **below**, sc in next 2 dc of previous row, ★ (sc, ch 2, sc) in Shell, (sc in next 2 dc of previous row, 2 dc in center of next 2-dc group 2 rows **below**) twice, skip next two 2-dc groups 2 rows **below**, (2 dc in center of next 2-dc group 2 rows **below**, sc in next 2 dc of previous row) twice; repeat from ★ 13 times **more**, (sc, ch 2, sc) in Shell, sc in next 2 dc of previous row, 2 dc in center of next 2-dc group 2 rows **below**, sc in next 2 dc of previous row, dc in center of next 2-dc group 2 rows **below**, dc in turning ch.

Rows 2 and 3: Ch 1, turn; working in previous row **only**, skip first st, ★ † sc in next 8 sts, (sc, ch 2, sc) in next ch-2 sp, sc in next 8 sts †, skip next 2 sts; repeat from ★13 times **more**, then repeat from † to † **once**.

Finish off.

BOTTOM EDGING

Row 1: Work in free loops of beginning ch as follows ***(Fig. 4, page 12)***:
Join Main Color with slip st in first st; ch 1, sc in same st and in next 8 sts, ★ skip next st (where Shell is worked), sc in next 8 sts, (sc, ch 2, sc) in next ch-2 space at peak, sc in next 8 sts; repeat from ★ 13 times **more**, skip next st, sc in last 9 sts.

Rows 2 and 3: Ch 1, turn; 2 sc in first sc, sc in next 7 sts, ★ skip next 2 sts, sc in next 8 sts, (sc, ch 2, sc) in next ch-2 sp at peak, sc in next 8 sts; repeat from ★ 13 times **more**, skip next 2 sts, sc in next 7 sts, 2 sc in last st.

Finish off.

Weave in all yarn ends.

STAINED GLASS

by Diana Nelson; Coal Valley, IL

Finished Size: Approximately 49" x 70" (124.5 cm x 178 cm)

MATERIALS

Worsted Weight Yarn, approximately:
Main Color - 25 ounces, (710 grams)
Contrasting Colors - 43 ounces, (1,220 grams) **total**
Crochet hook size G (4.5 mm)
or size needed for gauge

GAUGE: 3 Clusters = 2" (5 cm)

INSTRUCTIONS

With Main Color, ch 152 **loosely**.

Row 1: Sc in second ch from hook and in each ch across to last ch, sc in last ch until 2 loops remain on hook, with Contrasting Color, complete the sc ***(Fig. 5a, page 12)***; ch 1, turn: 151 sc.
Cut Main Color.

Row 2: Dc in first sc, ch 1, skip next sc, ★ work Cluster in next sc as follows: (work dc to last step) 3 times, YO ***(Fig. 2a)*** and draw through all 4 loops on hook **(Cluster made, *Fig. 2b*)**, ch 1, skip next sc; repeat from ★ across to last sc, dc in last sc changing to Main Color in same manner as before; ch 1, turn: 74 Clusters. Cut Contrasting Color.

Fig. 2a

Fig. 2b

Row 3: Sc in first dc, **long** sc in skipped sc of last Main Color row ***(Fig. 3)***, ★ sc in top of next Cluster, **long** sc in skipped sc of last Main Color row (between Clusters); repeat from ★ across, sc in last dc changing to Contrasting Color; ch 1, turn. Cut Main Color.

Fig. 3

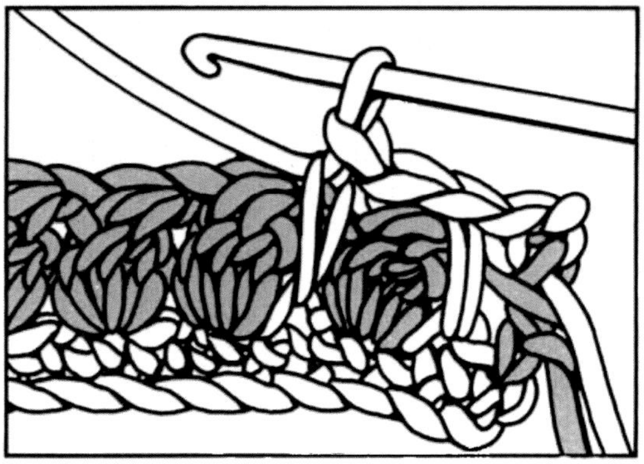

Repeat Rows 2 and 3 for pattern until Afghan is approximately 70" (178 cm) long, ending by working a Main Color Row. Do **not** ch 1 or change color at end of last row; finish off.

Weave in all yarn ends.

GENERAL INSTRUCTIONS

ABBREVIATIONS

ch(s)	chain(s)
cm	centimeters
dc	double crochet(s)
hdc	half double crochet(s)
mm	millimeters
Rnd	Round(s)
sc	single crochet(s)
sp(s)	space(s)
st(s)	stitch(es)
tr	treble crochet(s)
YO	yarn over

SYMBOLS & TERMS

★ — work instructions following ★ as many **more** times as indicated in addition to the first time.

† to † — work all instructions from first † to second † **as many** times as specified.

( ) — work enclosed instructions **as many** times as specified by the number immediately following **or** work all enclosed instructions in the stitch or space indicated **or** contains explanatory remarks.

CROCHET TERMINOLOGY		
UNITED STATES		INTERNATIONAL
slip stitch (slip st)	=	single crochet (sc)
single crochet (sc)	=	double crochet (dc)
half double crochet (hdc)	=	half treble crochet (htr)
double crochet (dc)	=	treble crochet (tr)
treble crochet (tr)	=	double treble crochet (dtr)
double treble crochet (dtr)	=	triple treble crochet (ttr)
triple treble crochet (tr tr)	=	quadruple treble crochet (qtr)
skip	=	miss

GAUGE

Correct gauge is essential for proper size of Afghan. Hook sizes given in instructions are merely guides and should never be used without first making a sample swatch approximately 6" (15 cm) square in the stitch, yarn, and hook specified. Then measure it, counting your stitches and rows carefully. If you have more stitches per inch than specified, try again with a larger size hook; if fewer, try again with a smaller size Keep trying until you find the size that will give you the specified gauge. **DO NOT HESITATE TO CHANGE HOOK SIZE TO OBTAIN CORRECT GAUGE.** Measure width of Afghan often to be sure your gauge remains consistent.

YARN

Since yardage per skein varies in different brands, you may wish to purchase more than the specified amount to ensure having sufficient yarn of the same dye lot.

FINISHING

Good finishing techniques make a big difference in the quality of your Afghan. Make a habit of taking care of loose ends as you work. To keep loose ends from showing, always weave them back through several stitches or work over them. When ends are secure, clip them off close to work.

FREE LOOPS OF A CHAIN

When instructed to work in free loops of a chain, work in loop indicated by arrow ***(Fig. 4)***.

Fig. 4

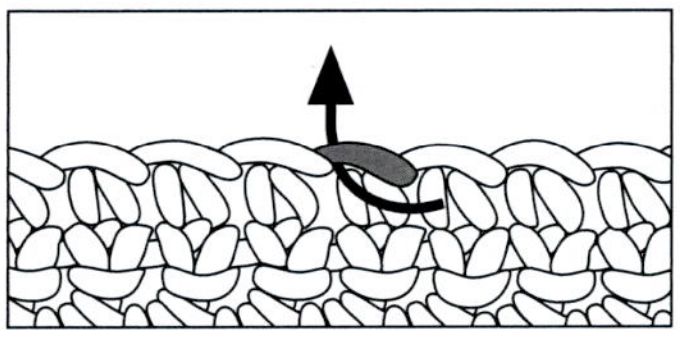

CHANGING COLORS

Work the last stitch to within one step of completion, hook new yarn ***(Figs. 5a or 5b)*** and draw through all loops on hook.

Fig. 5a

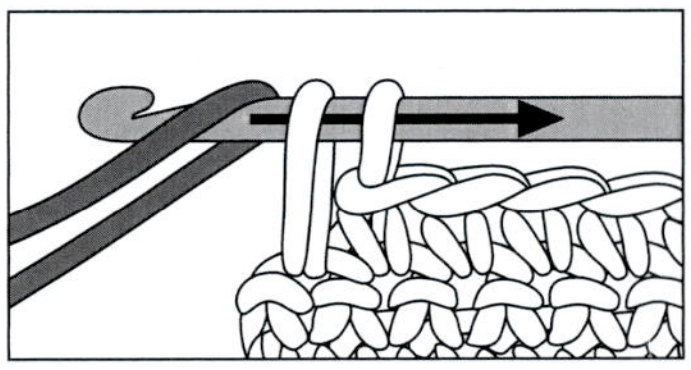

Fig. 5b

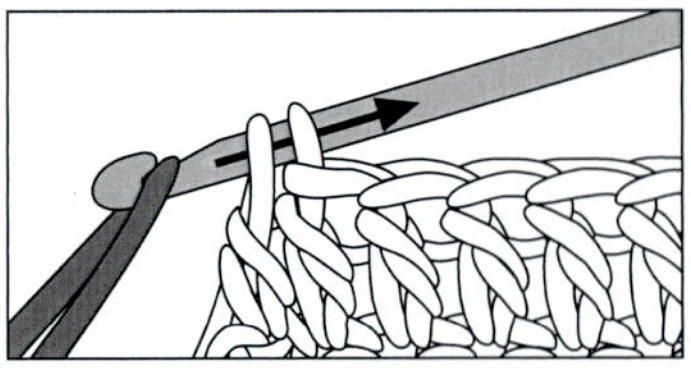

CROCHET HOOKS																	
U.S.	B-1	C-2	D-3	E-4	F-5	G-6	7	H-8	I-9	J-10	K-10½	L-11	M/N-13	N/P-15	P/Q	Q	S
Metric - mm	2.25	2.75	3.25	3.5	3.75	4	4.5	5	5.5	6	6.5	8	9	10	15	16	19

Made in U.S.A.